The Canine Companion:

Quotes for Dog Lovers

Edited by Heather Russell-Revesz

BARNES
& NOBLE
BOOKS

NEW YORK

Compilation copyright © 2004 by Barnes & Noble, Inc.

2004 Barnes & Noble Books

ISBN 0-7607-6142-6

Printed and bound in the United States of America

04 05 06 07 HC 9 8 7 6 5 4 3 2 1

APPROXIMATELY 135,000 YEARS AGO, DOGS SPLIT off from wolves (genetically speaking), and formed a bond with humans. Since then, dogs have worked for us, played with us, and lived up to the nickname Man's Best Friend (or Woman's Best Friend, as the case may be).

There is something in the expressiveness of their eyes, the playful wag of the tail, the welcome home bark that touches everyone who has ever lived with or loved a dog. They have become woven into our culture: What feeling person wouldn't cry at the end of *Old Yeller*? Who didn't think Lassie was smarter than any of the humans she helped out? How could you not be charmed by Lady and The Tramp eating a romantic dinner featuring a bowl of spaghetti?

Dogs, both fictional and flesh-and-bone, touch a chord within our hearts. Loyalty, fidelity, friendship, unselfish love—these are all words that come up again and again when uncovering what we humans have to say about our 135,000 year-old friendship with dogs.

A Dog Is...

A dog hath true love
A dog hath right good understanding
A wise dog knoweth all things
A dog hath force and kindliness
A dog hath mettle and is comely
A dog is in all things seemly.
A knowing dog thinketh no evil
A dog hath a memory that forgeteth not
I say unto you again a dog forsaketh not his duty
Hath might and cunning therewith
And a great brave heart.

—GARE DE LA VIGNE, "Poème sur la Chasse"

Dogs are our link to paradise. They don't know evil or jealousy or discontent. To sit with a dog on a hillside on a glorious afternoon is to be back in Eden, where doing nothing was not boring—it was peace.

—Milan Kundera

A dog has the soul of a philosopher.

—Plato

Dog. A kind of additional or subsidiary Deity designed to catch the overflow and surplus of the world's worship.

—Ambrose Bierce, *The Devil's Dictionary*

You may drive a dog off the King's armchair, and it will climb into the preacher's pulpit; he views the world unmoved, unembarrassed, unabashed.

—JEAN DE LA BRUYÈRE, "Of Personal Merit"

I myself have known some profoundly thoughtful dogs.

—JAMES THURBER

The disposition of noble dogs is to be gentle with people they know and the opposite with those they don't know… How, then, can the dog be anything other than a lover of learning since it defines what's its own and what's alien.

—PLATO

To call him a dog hardly seems to do him justice, though in as much as he had four legs, a tail and barked, I admit he was, to all outward appearances. But to those of us who knew him well, he was a perfect gentleman.

—HERMIONE GINGOLD

Among God's creatures two, the dog and the guitar, have taken all the sizes and all the shapes, in order not to be separated from the man.

—ANDRÈS SEGOVIA, *New York Times*, 1964

A hounde is trewe to his lord or his mayster, and of good lover or vrey.

—EDWARD, SECOND DUKE OF YORK,
"Mayster of the Game"

Loyalty

He is loyalty itself. He has taught me the meaning of devotion... His head on my knee can heal my human hurts.

—GENE HILL, Tears and Laughter

That one true heart was left behind!
What feeling do we ever find
To equal among human kind
A dog's fidelity!

—THOMAS HARDY,
"Ah, Are You Digging on My Grave?"

But thinks, admitted to that equal sky,
His faithful dog shall bear him company.

—ALEXANDER POPE, *Essay on Man*

Histories are more full of examples of the fidelity of dogs than of friends.

—ALEXANDER POPE

He is very imprudent, a dog is. He never makes it his business to inquire whether you are in the right or in the wrong, never bothers as to whether you are going up or down upon life's ladder, never asks whether you are rich or poor, silly or wise, sinner or saint. Come luck or misfortune, good repute or bad, honor or shame, he is going to stick to you, to comfort you, guard you, and give his life for you.

—JEROME K. JEROME

A dog will never forget the crumb thou gave him, though thou mayst afterwards throw a hundred stones at his head.

—SA'DI

If I sit down on a bench he is at my side at once and takes up a position on one of my feet. For it is a law of his being that he only runs about when I am in motion too; that when I settle down he follows suit.

—THOMAS MANN, "A Man and His Dog"

While I think I would have enjoyed the company of many different dogs, I believe that the depth of my feeling for Rose in particular comes from the fact that she is, in matters of intelligence, loyalty, and affection, an extraordinary animal.

—ANNE PATCHETT, "This Dog's Life"

Recollect that the Almighty, who gave the dog to be companion of our pleasures and our toils, hath invested him with a nature noble and incapable of deceit.

—SIR WALTER SCOTT, *The Talisman*

You ask of my Companions. Hills—Sir—and the Sundown—and a Dog—large as myself, that my father bought me—they are better than Beings—because they know—but do not tell...

—EMILY DICKINSON,
letter to Colonel T. W. Higginson, 1892

I have found that when you are deeply troubled there are things you get from the silent devoted companionship of a dog that you can get from no other source.

—DORIS DAY

Why We Love Them

Buy a pup and your money will buy love unflinching.

—RUDYARD KIPLING

I think dogs are the most amazing creatures. For me they are the role model for being alive.

—GILDA RADNER

Puppies are nature's remedy for feeling unloved... plus numerous other aliments of life.

—Richard Allan Palm

It doesn't matter what it is, what crime against Dog I have committed, she always forgives me. She doesn't even appear to think about it. One minute she's noting my odd behavior, the next, if I make a move toward her, she's licking my hand. As if to say, Gosh, I'm so glad you're yourself again, and you're back!

—Alice Walker, "Crimes Against Dog"

We love dogs because they show us how to live with utmost simplicity...

—Erica Jong, "A Woman's Best Friend"

"Do you have a dog?" I said to a thin elderly man on arm crutches, with a hearing aid in each ear. He had arrived unaccompanied.

"No," he said, "but I'm in love with a dog." He proceeded to tell me about the black Lab next door who came to visit him every day. Tears formed at the edges of his eyes.

—Louise Bernikow, "The Dog Is a Ham"

The emotional bonds between people and their dogs remain private and powerful, often unhindered by contractions or reality, free to grow and expand in ways outsiders can never fully grasp.

—Jon Katz, "Donna and Harry"

The great pleasure of a dog is that you may make a fool of yourself with him and not only will he not scold you, but he will make a fool of himself too.

—SAMUEL BUTLER, "Higgledy-Piggledy"

Happiness is a warm puppy!

—CHARLES SCHULTZ, *Peanuts*

I lie on my burgundy velvet couch, smelly with dog and hair everywhere, with Ralph and Bronwyn fighting for the curved space between my legs or the soft pad of my belly, and I realize that I am happier than I have ever been.

—MARGARET CHO, "The New Girl"

The gift which I am sending you is called a dog, and is in fact the most precious and valuable possession of mankind.

—Theodorius Gaza, "Canis Laudatio"

Pray steal me not, I'm Mrs. Dingley's, whose heart in this four-footed thing lies.

—Jonathan Swift,
inscription on the collar of a lapdog

And They Love Us Back

To his dog, every man is Napoleon; hence the constant popularity of dogs.

—ALDOUS HUXLEY

It is by muteness that a dog becomes for one so utterly beyond value; with him one is at peace, where words play no torturing tricks. Those are the moments that I think are precious to a dog when, with his adoring soul coming through his eyes, he feels that you are really thinking of him.

—JOHN GALSWORTHY, "Memories"

You have seen that look. The way a young painter looks at a Rembrandt or Titian. The way Liz Taylor looks at Richard Burton. The way Zsa Zsa looks at mink. That's how a poodle looks at its master.

—Jacqueline Susann

Of course what he most intensely dreams of is being taken out on walks, and the more you are able to indulge him the more will he adore you and the more all the latent beauty of his nature will come out.

—Henry James, (on his dog Max)

A dog is the only thing on this earth that loves you more than he loves himself.

—Josh Billings (Henry Wheeler Shaw),
American humorist

A dog without a master is a forlorn creature; no society of other dogs seems to console him; he wanders about disconsolate, till he finds some human being to whom to attach himself, and then he's a made dog—he pads about with an air of dignity, like a dog that is settled in life.

—HARRIET BEECHER STOWE,
"Our Dogs and Other Stories"

Dogs watch for us faithfully. They love and worship their masters. They hate strangers,. Their power of tracking scent is extraordinary. Great is their keenness in the chase—what can all this mean but that they were made for man's advantage?

—CICERO, "De Oficius"

If a dog doesn't put you first where are you both? In what relation? A dog needs God. It lives by your glances, your wishes. It even shares your humor. This happens about the fifth year. If it doesn't happen you are only keeping an animal.

—ENID BAGNOLD, *Autobiography*

For take an Example of a Dog: And mark what a Generosity and Courage he will put on, when he finds himself maintained by a Man; Who to him is in stead of a God, or Melior Natura; which courage is manifestly such as that creature without that confidence of a better nature then his own, could never attain.

—FRANCIS BACON, "Essay on Atheisme"

Living with Dogs

Living with a dog is messy—like living with an idealist.

—H. L. MENCKEN, *A Mencken Chrestomathy*

In order to really enjoy a dog, one doesn't merely try to train him to be semihuman. The point of it is to open oneself to the possibility of becoming partly a dog.

—EDWARD HOAGLAND, "Dogs and the Tug of Life"

I would recommend to those persons who are inclined to stagnate, whose blood is beginning to thicken sluggishly in their veins, to try keeping four dogs, two of which are puppies.

—ELIZABETH VON ARNUM

If you don't have a dog—at least one—there is not necessarily anything wrong with you, but there may be something wrong with your life.

—VINCENT VAN GOGH

'Tis sweet to hear the watch-dog's honest bark
Bay deep-mouth'd welcome as we draw near
    home,
'Tis sweet to know there is an eye will mark our
    coming,
and look brighter when we come.

—GEORGE GORDON, LORD BYRON

Once in a great while...the right person is fortunate enough to get the right dog, to have the time to take care of it, to connect with it in a profound way.

—JON KATZ, *A Dog Year: Twelve Months, Four Dogs and Me*

It is quaint, cozy, and amusing to feel him sitting upon my foot and penetrating it with the feverish glow of his body. A sense of gaiety and sympathy fills my bosom, as always when I am abandoned to him and to his idea of things.

—THOMAS MANN, *Bashan and I*

I have discovered the thrill of anticipating a dog, the excitement in the mere idea of a dog.

—ELENA SIGMAN, "The Existence of Dog"

What's more, dogs rarely mind your joining them at rest. Nor do they often refuse the request to stop whatever else they might be doing to join you at rest. People aren't as accommodating; we're fidgety, physically and psychologically. Human naps are usually taken solo.

—MICHAEL J. ROSEN, "Sleeping with the Pack"

For me a house or an apartment becomes a home when you add one set of four legs, a happy tail, and that indescribable measure of love we call a dog.

—ROGER CARAS, former President of the ASPCA

Friendship

Then the Man walked up he said, "What is Wild Dog doing here?" And the Woman said, "His name is not Wild Dog any more, but the First Friend, because he will be our friend for always and always and always."

—R<small>UDYARD</small> K<small>IPLING</small>

Extraordinary creature! So close a friend, and yet so remote.

—T<small>HOMAS</small> M<small>ANN</small>, "A Man and his Dog"

I, who had had my heart full for hours, took advantage of an early moment of solitude, to cry in it very bitterly. Suddenly a little hairy head thrust itself from behind my pillow into my face, rubbing its ears and nose against me in a responsive agitation, and drying the tears as they came.

—Elizabeth Barrett Browning

The dog is the only animal that is capable of disinterested affection. It is the only creature that regards the human being in his compassion, and follows him as his friend; the only one that seems to possess a natural desire to be useful to him, or from a spontaneous impulse attaches himself to man.

—William Youatt, "The Dog"

Pug is come!—come to fill up the void left by false and narrow-hearted friends. I see already that he is without envy, hatred, or malice—that he will betray no secrets, and feel neither pain at my success nor pleasure in my chagrin.

—GEORGE ELIOT

I needed a companion on whom to lavish my overflowing, if at times destructible, affection. I needed a dog.

—ALICE WALKER, "Crimes Against Dog"

There are three faithful friends—an old wife, an old dog, and ready money.

—BENJAMIN FRANKLIN, *Poor Richards' Almanac*

The one absolute, unselfish friend that man can have in this selfish world—the one that never deserts him, the one that never proves ungrateful or treacherous—is his dog.

GEORGE GRAHAM VEST, Senate speech, 1884

My leader, Pete, was a fine dog. When he would come and lay his head on my knee and look up into my eyes, I could feel the love and faith he could not put into words.

—ADMIRAL RICHARD BYRD, "By Dog Sled for Byrd"

Dogs In Poetry

Pollicle dogs and cats all must
Jellicle cats and dogs all must
Like undertakers, come to dust.
Here a little dog I pause
Heaving up my prior paws,
Pause, and sleep endlessly.

—T. S. ELIOT, "Five-Finger Exercises"

The dog barks, the caravan passes on.
The words had a sort of bloom on them
But were weightless, carrying past what was
    being said.

—JOHN ASHBERY, "Grand Galop"

An earthly dog of the carriage breed;
Who, having failed of the modern speed,
Now asked asylum and I was stirred
To be the one so dog-preferred.

—Robert Frost, "One More Brevity"

A dog starved at his master's gate
Predicts the ruin of the state.

—William Blake, "Auguries of Innocence"

The little dog lay curled and did not rise
But slept the deeper as the ashes rose
And found the people incomplete...

—Richard Wilbur, "Year's End"

Old Mother Hubbard
Went to the cupboard
To get her poor dog a bone:
But when she got there
The cupboard was bare,
And so the poor dog had none.

        —MOTHER GOOSE, "Old Mother Hubbard"

Lately, I've been accustomed to the way
The ground opens up and envelops me
Each time I go out to walk the dog.

        —LE ROI JONES (AMIRI BARAKA)
        "Preface to a Twenty Volume Suicide Note"

In the nightmare of the dark
All the dogs of Europe bark

        —W. H. AUDEN, "In Memory of W. B. Yeats"

The old dog barks backward without getting up.
I can remember when he was a pup.

—ROBERT FROST, "II. The Span of Life"

i have just come from a swell
dog show he said i have
been lunching off a dog that was
worth at least one hundred
dollars a pound

—DON MARQUIS, "the merry fleas"

Writers and Dogs

Charley likes to get up early, and he likes me to get up early too. And why shouldn't he? Right after his breakfast he goes back to sleep.

—JOHN STEINBECK, *Travels with Charley*

Sentences and paragraphs. Sentences are not emotional but paragraphs are. I can say that as often as I like and it always remains as it is, something that is. I said I found this out first in listening to Basket my dog drinking. And anybody listening to any dog's drinking will see what I mean.

GERTRUDE STEIN, "Poetry and Grammar"

Oh Lord! I forgot to tell you I have got a little dog, and Mr C. has accepted it with amiability. To be sure, when he comes down gloomy in the morning or comes in wearied from his week, the infatuated little beast dances round him on its hind legs, as I ought to do and can't; and he feels flattered and surprised by such unwonted capers to his honour and glory.

—JANE CARLYLE, letter to John Forster, 1849

He nosed his way from smell to smell; the rough, the smooth, the dark, the golden.

—VIRGINIA WOOLF, "Flush"

"It is of the highest importance in the art of detection to be able to recognize out of a number of facts which are incidental and which are vital.... I would call your attention to the curious incident of the dog in the night-time."

"The dog did nothing in the night-time."

"That was the curious incident," remarked Sherlock Holmes.

—Sir Arthur Conan Doyle,
The Memoirs of Sherlock Holmes

Let sleeping dogs lie—who wants to rouse 'em?

—Charles Dickens, *David Copperfield*

Dogskull, dogsniff, eyes on the ground, nose to one great goal. Ah, poor dogsbody. Here lies dogsbody's body.

—James Joyce, *Ulysses*

I am his Highness' dog at Kew;
Pray tell me, sir, whose dog are you?

—ALEXANDER POPE, epigram engraved on the collar
of a Dog which I Gave to His Royal Highness

I am I because my little dog knows me but, creatively speaking the little dog knowing that you are you and your recognizing that he knows, that is what destroys creation. That is what makes school.

—GERTRUDE STEIN, *What Are Masterpieces and
Why Are There So Few of Them*

Dogs vs. Cats

A dog will make eye contact. A cat will, too, but a cat's eyes don't even look entirely warm-blooded to me, whereas a dog's eyes look human except less guarded. A dog will look at you as if to say, "What do you want me to do for you? I'll do anything for you." Whether a dog can in fact, do anything for you if you don't have sheep (I never have) is another matter. The dog is willing.

—Roy Blount, Jr. "Dogs Vis-A-Vis Cats"

If a dog jumps into your lap it is because he is fond of you; but if a cat does the same thing it is because your lap is warmer.

—ALFRED NORTH WHITEHEAD

You call to a dog and a dog will break its neck to get to you. Dogs just want to please. Call to a cat and its attitude is, "What's in it for me?"

—LEWIS GRIZZARD, "Pet Peeves"

Cats are the ultimate narcissists. You can tell this because of all the time they spend on personal grooming. Dogs aren't like this. A dog's idea of personal grooming is to roll in a pile of dead fish. Dogs spend their time thinking about doing good deeds for their masters, or sleeping.

—JAMES GORMAN, "The Sociobiology of Humor in Cats and Dogs"

The dog is mentioned in the Bible eighteen times—the cat not even once.

—W. E. Farbstein, quoted in *Mondo Canine*

Women and cats will do as they please, and men and dogs should relax and get used to the idea.

—Robert A. Heinlein

Artists like cats, soldiers like dogs.

—Desmond Morris

Sometimes we met a wrecker with his cart and dog,—and his dog's faint bark at us wayfarers, heard through the roaring of the surf, sounded ridiculously faint. To see a little trembling dainty-footed cur stand on the margin of the ocean, and ineffectually bark at a beach-bird, amid the roar of the Atlantic! Come with design to bark at a whale, perchance! That sound will do for farm-yards. All the dogs looked out of place there, naked and as if shuddering at the vastness; and I thought that they would not have been there had it not been for the countenance of their masters. Still less could you think of a cat bending her steps that way, and shaking her wet foot over the Atlantic; yet even this happens sometimes, they tell me.

—Henry David Thoreau, *Cape Cod*

What They're Thinking

Yesterday I was a dog. Today I'm a dog. Tomorrow I'll probably still be a dog. Sigh! There's so little hope for advancement.

—SNOOPY, *Peanuts* created by Charles Schulz

I've seen a look in dogs' eyes, a quickly vanishing look of amazed contempt, and I am convinced that basically dogs think humans are nuts.

—JOHN STEINBECK

Dogs feel very strongly that they should always go with you in the car, in case the need should arise for them to bark violently at nothing right in your ear.

—DAVE BARRY

When people try to name the Tao, they never succeed. And when people call me "the dog," I don't pay much attention.

—WILSON THE PUG (with Nancy Levine),
The Tao of Pug

You can say any foolish thing to a dog, and the dog will give you a look that says, "My God, you're right! I never would've thought of that!"'

—DAVE BARRY

If you are a dog and your owner suggests that you wear a sweater…suggest that he wear a tail.

—FRAN LEBOWITZ, "Pointers for Pets"

A reasonable amount o' fleas is good fer a dog—keeps him from broodin' over bein' a dog, mebbe.

—EDWARD NOYES WESTCOTT, *David Harum*

I don't think he has any idea he's a dog, not really. Of course, he thinks he has a rather odd figure for a man.

—PAMELA FITZGERALD (Ruth Hussey), *The Uninvited*

Ever consider what dogs must think of us? I mean, here we come back from a grocery store with the most amazing haul—chicken, pork, half a cow. They must think we're the greatest hunters on earth!

—ANNE TYLER

A dog desires more affection than his dinner. Well, almost.

—CHARLOTTE GRAY

A Noble Creature

If you pick up a starving dog and make him prosperous, he will not bite you. This is the principal difference between a dog and a man.

—MARK TWAIN, "Pudd'nhead Wilson's Calendar"

If I have any beliefs about immortality, it is that certain dogs I have known will go to heaven, and very, very few persons.

—JAMES THURBER

If a dog will not come to you after having looked you in the face, you should go home and examine your conscience.

—WOODROW WILSON

So many get reformed through religion. I got reformed through my dogs.

—LINDA BASQUETTE

The censure of a dog is something no man can stand.

—CHRISTOPHER MORLEY

I can train any dog in 5 minutes. It's training the owner that takes longer.

—BARBARA WOODHOUSE

Don't accept your dog's admiration as conclusive evidence that you are wonderful.

—ANN LANDERS

Dogs love their friends and bite their enemies, quite unlike people, who are incapable of pure love and always have to mix love and hate.

—SIGMUND FREUD

The more I see of men, the more I like dogs.

—MADAME DE STAEL

The dog has seldom been successful in pulling man up to its level of sagacity, but man has frequently dragged the dog down to his.

—JAMES THURBER

Heaven goes by favor. If it went by merit, you would stay out and your dog would go in.

—MARK TWAIN

Dogs At Work

Their tails are high and tongues awag—the twin banners of sled dog contentment.

—Clara Germani, on Alaskan Huskies in the Iditarod sled dog race

The shepherd is the brain behind the dog's brain,
But his control of dog, like dog's of sheep
Is never absolute—that's the beauty of it.

—Cecil Day Lewis, "Sheepdog Trials in Hyde Park"

Back at Guiding Eyes she distinguishes herself by passing the famous "jelly doughnut test." The trainers have placed doughnuts and slices of pepperoni pizza around the training center. As we walk through the hallways, she pays them no attention and even guides me around them!

I suspect this dog reads the encyclopedia in her spare time.

—STEPHEN KUUSISTO, "Blind Date"

The hounding of a dog pursuing a fox or other animal in the horizon may have first suggested the notes of the hunting-horn to alternate with and relieve the lungs of the dog. This natural bugle long resounded in the woods of the ancient world before the horn was invented.

—HENRY DAVID THOREAU,
"A Week on the Concord and Merrimack Rivers"

Few working dogs worked harder than Harry. Much of the work that dogs are being asked to do in contemporary America involves not guarding livestock or hunting birds, but tending to human beings and their emotional needs.

—Jon Katz, "Donna and Harry"

Montmorency [the dog] came and sat on things just when they were wanted to be packed. He put his leg into the jam, and he worried the teaspoons, and he pretended that the lemons were rats, and got into the hamper and killed three of them.

—Jerome K. Jerome, "Three Men In a Boat"

A good snow machine will cost $2,000 and last four to five years. With dogs, you've got regenerative powers. Snow machines don't have pups.

—Lou Schultz, Alaskan Husky trainer

In shapes and forms of dogges; of which there are but two sorts that are usefull for man's profit, which are the mastiffe and the little whippet, or house dogge; all the rest are for pleasure and recreation.

—JOHN TAYLOR

To think that one small dog could stand for so much in the life of a human being, not only in his usual role of companion but as his eyes, sword, shield and buckle! How many humans could fill those roles with the same uncomplaining devotion and untiring fidelity? Darned few, I think.

—DOROTHY EUSTIS, "The Seeing Eye" 1927

The Bard on Dogs

Let Hercules himself do what he may,
The cat will mew and dog will have his day.

—WILLIAM SHAKESPEARE, *Hamlet*,
act 5, scene 1

LEAR: Thou hast seen a farmer's dog bark at a
beggar?
GLOUCESTER: Ay, sir.
LEAR: And the creature run from the cur? There
thou mightst behold the great image of
authority: a dog's obeyed in office.

—WILLIAM SHAKESPEARE, *King Lear,*
act 4, scene 6

Cry "Havoc!" and let slip the dogs of war.

—WILLIAM SHAKESPEARE, *Julius Caesar*,
act 3, scene 1

Thou call'st me dog before thou hadst a cause,
But since I am a dog, beware my fangs.

—WILLIAM SHAKESPEARE, *The Merchant of Venice*,
act 3, scene 3

He's a very dog to the commonalty.

—WILLIAM SHAKESPEARE, *Coriolanus*,
act 1, scene 1

I had rather hear my dog bark at a crow than a
man swear he loves me.

> —WILLIAM SHAKESPEARE, *Much Ado About Nothing,*
> act 1, scene 1

Truly, I would not hang a dog by my will, much
more a man who hath any honesty in him.

> —WILLIAM SHAKESPEARE, *Much Ado About Nothing,*
> act 3, scene 3

As familiar with me as my dog.

> —WILLIAM SHAKESPEARE, *Henry IV, Part 2,*
> act 2, scene 2

I had rather be a dog, and bay the moon,
Than such a Roman.

> —WILLIAM SHAKESPEARE, *Julius Caesar,*
> act 4, scene 3

Talks as familiarly of roaring lions
As maids of thirteen do of puppy-dogs!

—WILLIAM SHAKESPEARE, *King John*,
act 2, scene 1

I am Sir Oracle
And when I ope my lips let no dog bark.

—WILLIAM SHAKESPEARE, *The Merchant of Venice*,
act 1, scene 7

Mine enemy's dog
Though he had bit me, should have stood that
    night
Against my fire.

—WILLIAM SHAKESPEARE, *King Lear*,
act 4, scene 7

All that I have to say, is, to tell you
that the lanthorn is the moon; I
the man in the moon; this
thorn-bush, my thorn-bush; and
this dog, my dog.

—WILLIAM SHAKESPEARE, *A Midsummer Night's Dream*,
act 5, scene 1

The little dogs and all,
Tray, Blanche, and Sweetheart, see
They bark at me.

—WILLIAM SHAKESPEARE, *King Lear*,
act 3, scene 6

Sir, he's a good dog, and a fair dog; can there be
more said?

—WILLIAM SHAKESPEARE, *Merry Wives of Windsor*,
act 1, scene 1

Famous Dogs

You can't ask Lassie questions, Mom. She'll only bark at you.

—TIMMY (JON PROVOST), from the TV show *Lassie*

I'm the dog. I'm well read and have a diverse stock portfolio. But I'm not above eating grass clippings and regurgitating them on the rug.

—STEWIE, taunting Brian (the family dog), *The Family Guy*

I think Eminem should take relax a little. I mean, my mom's a bitch too, but I don't sing songs about it.

—Triumph the Insult Comic Dog,
Late Night With Conan O'Brien

Toto, I've a feeling we're not in Kansas anymore.

—Dorothy (Judy Garland), *The Wizard of Oz*,
screenplay by Noel Langley

That's the only dog I know who can smell someone just thinking about food.

—Charlie Brown on Snoopy

This man had saved his life, which was something; but, further, he was the ideal master. Other men saw to the welfare of their dogs from a sense of duty and business expediency; he saw to the welfare of his as if they were his children, because he could not help it.

—BUCK, from Jack London's *The Call of the Wild*

It was Old Yeller who saved me. He flung himself between me and the killer hogs. He yelled with pain as the savage tusks ripped into him. He took the awful punishment meant for me. He gave me that one-in-a-hundred chance to get free. I took it.

—FRED GIPSON, *Old Yeller*

Doggy Politics

[My dog] can bark like a congressman, fetch like an aide, beg like a press secretary and play dead like a receptionist when the phone rings.

—GERALD B. H. SOLOMON, U.S. Congressman, entry in contest to identify Capitol Hill's Great American Dog

If you want a friend in Washington, get a dog.

—HARRY S TRUMAN

My advice to any diplomat who wants to have a good press is to have two or three kids and a dog.

—Carl T. Rowan, Jr., U.S. Ambassador to Finland

These Republican leaders have not been content with attacks on me, or my wife, or on my sons. No, not content with that, they now include my little dog Fala. Well, of course I don't resent attacks, but Fala does resent them. You know, Fala is Scotch, and being a Scottie, learning that the Republican fiction writers in Congress and out had concocted a story that I had left him behind on the Aleutian Islands and had sent a destroyer back to find him—at a cost to the tax payers of two or three, or eight or twenty million dollars—his Scotch soul was furious. He has not been the same dog since.

—Franklin D. Roosevelt, address to the Teamster's Union September 23, 1944

I love a dog. He does nothing for political reasons.

—WILL ROGERS

...it was a little cocker spaniel dog in a crate that he had sent all the way from Texas. Black and white spotted. And our little girl, Tricia, the six-year-old, named it Checkers. And you know, the kids love the dog, and I just want to say this right now, that regardless of what they say about it, we're gonna keep it.

—RICHARD MILHOUS NIXON, "Checkers" speech, September 23, 1952

I'll be with you until the last dog dies.

—WILLIAM JEFFERSON CLINTON, campaign speech, 1992

Loss

Grief can not drive him away;
He is gentle, he is kind—
I shall never, never find
A better friend than old dog Tray!

—Stephen Collins Foster, "Old Dog Tray"

The misery of keeping a dog is his dying so soon.
But, to be sure, if he lived for fifty years and then
died, what would become of me?

—Sir Walter Scott

Near this spot are deposited the remains of one who possessed Beauty without Vanity, Strength without Insolence, Courage without Ferocity, and all the Virtues of Man without his Vices. This praise, which would be unmeaning Flattery, if inscribed over human ashes, is but a just Tribute to the Memory of BOATSWAIN, a Dog.

—George Gordon, Lord Byron

I once heard a woman who'd lost her dog say that she felt as though a color were suddenly missing from her world: The dog had introduced to her field of vision some previously unavailable hue, and without the dog, that color was gone.

—Caroline Knapp, "The Color of Joy"

Dogs come into our lives to teach us about love and loyalty. They depart to teach us about loss.

—Erica Jong, "A Woman's Best Friend"

Where can I go
without my mount
all eager and quick
How will I know
in thicket ahead
is danger or treasure
when Body my good
bright dog is dead.

—MARY SWANSON, "Question"

Old dog Tray's ever faithful; Be with me, Beauty,
    for the fire is dying;
My dog and I are old, too old for roving.

—JOHN MANSFIELD, "On Growing Old"

It is a terrible thing for an old woman to outlive
her dogs.

—TENNESSEE WILLIAMS, *Camino Real*

Proverbs and Sayings

Better to be a dog in times of peace than a human being in times of trouble.

—CHINESE PROVERB

A living dog is better than a dead lion.

—ECCLESIASTES 9:4

Pray thee let me and my fellow have
A haire of the dog that bit us last night

—JOHN HEYWOOD, *Proverbes*

A good dog does not block the road.

—CHINESE PROVERB

The greatest love is a mother's;
Then comes a dog's,
Then comes a sweetheart's.

—POLISH PROVERB

She saved for tomorrow. When she was asleep, the dog ate up her flour.

—PUNJABI PROVERB

Killing the dog does not cure the bite.

—Abraham Lincoln

In fact, now I come to think of it, do we decide questions, at all? We decide answers, no doubt: but surely the questions decide us? It is the dog, you know, that wags the tail—not the tail that wags the dog.

—Lewis Carroll, letter to Marion Richards, 1886

Keep running after a dog, and he will never bite you.

—Francois Rabelais

When a dog bites a man, that is not news, because it happens so often. But if a man bites a dog, that is news.

—Frank M. O'Brien, in John B. Bogart's
The Story of The (New York) Sun

A dog hath a day.

—John Heywood, *Proverbes*

Young blood must have its course, lad,
And every dog his day.

—Charles Kingsley, "Water Babies"

Qui me amat, amat et canem meum.
[Who loves me, also loves my dog.]

—Bernard of Clairvaux

Is thy servant a dog, that he
Should do this great thing?

—II Kings 8:13

He is so poor that he could not keep a dog.

—Longus, *Daphnis and Chloe*

Mad dogs and Englishmen go out in the midday
sun.

—Noel Coward

Cave canem.
[Beware of the dog]

—Proverb

Bad Dog!

But my greatest delight is to take a good bite
At a calf that is plump and delicious;
And if I indulge in a bite at a bulge,
Let's hope you won't think me too vicious.

> —Dylan Thomas,
> "The Song of the Mischievous Dog"

I'm a lean dog, a keen dog,
A wild dog, and lone.

> —Irene Rutherford McLeod, "Lone Dog"

Dooley's about a hundred pounds of white-and-liver-freckled, manic, goofy off-bird dog. He showed up one winter morning, practically crawling across the front yard, as submissive as he could be. But he has the personality of an old drunk: If he's not telling the other dogs how much he loves them—inviting them over to share his bowl—then he's going for the jugular.

—GEORGE SINGLETON, "Why We Don't Play Chess"

This dog and man at first were friends;
But when a pique began,
The dog, to gain some private ends,
Went mad and bit the man
The man recovered of the bile,
The dog it was that died.

—OLIVER GOLDSMITH, "The Vicar of Wakefield"

And in that town a dog was found,
As many dogs there be,
Both mongrel, puppy, whelp, and hound,
And curs of low degree.

—OLIVER GOLDSMITH,
"Elegy on the Death of a Mad Dog"

The most affectionate creature in the world is a wet dog.

—AMBROSE BIERCE

You ain't nothin' but a hound dog
Cryin' all the time
Well, you ain't never caught a rabbit
And you ain't no friend of mine.

—ELVIS PRESLEY, "Hound Dog,"
lyrics by Mike Stoller

The gingham dog went "Bow-wow-wow,"
And the calico cat replied "Mee-ow."
The air was littered, an hour or so,
With bits of gingham and calico.

—Eugene Field, "The Duel"

Dogs and Children

The dog was created especially for children. He is the god of frolic.

—Henry Ward Beecher

But a dog teaches a boy fidelity, perseverance, and to turn around three times before lying down—very important traits in times like these. In fact, just as soon as a dog comes along who, in addition to these qualities, also knows when to buy and sell stocks, he can be moved right up to the boy's bedroom and the boy can sleep in the dog house.

—Robert Benchley, "Your Boy and His Dog"

Teddy's job was to save Rosette's spirit. She has dog love threading through her veins from some ancestor, dog love wound tightly around her heart like the branching arteries displayed in her encyclopedia... Teddy was hers alone. She slept in his dog bed, and he slept on her small fold-out couch in the living room. He walked her to pre-school with me every day, and her class, The Cute Kittens, mobbed him. He never barked or growled or even moved.

—SUSAN STRAIGHT,
"Brave and Noble is the Preschool Dog"

Dachshunds are ideal dogs for small children, and they are already stretched and pulled to such a length that the child cannot do much harm one way or the other.

—ROBERT BENCHLEY

The dog hesitated for a moment, but presently made some little advances with his tail. The child put out his hand and called him. In an apologetic manner the dog came close, and the two had an interchange of friendly pattings and waggles.

—STEPHEN CRANE

Every puppy should have a boy.

—ERMA BOMBECK

When I was very little lad, I had a very little dog called Punch. I saw to his feeding myself.

—JACK LONDON, *The Road*

Newfoundland dogs are good to save children from drowning, but you must have a pond of water handy and a child, or else there will be no profit in boarding a Newfoundland.

–JOSH BILLINGS (HENRY WHEELER SHAW) "Essays"

Who Wouldn't Love a Dog?

Anyone who hates children and dogs can't be all bad.

—Attributed to W. C. FIELDS

I loathe people who keep dogs. They are cowards who haven't got the guts to bite people themselves.

—AUGUST STRINDBERG, "A Madman's Diary"

If we eliminated the dog from our lives, nothing much would happen to our ecology. Independent of man, the dog is a vandal. With man, he does a little sheep-herding, a little watch-dogging. He helps law enforcement officers control the troublesome ghetto-dwellers and protest marchers. He sniffs out "hash" and "grass." He goes out on weekends and helps man murder other forms of life for pleasure. But mostly he is just an adjunct to man's ego....

—PAUL COREY,
"Cat-Watching in the Cybernetic Age"

The paper boy curses the dog through the latched screen door.

—MASON COOLEY, *City Aphorisms*

It is just this rage for consideration that has betrayed the dog into his satellite position as the friend of man. The cat, an animal of franker appetites, preserves his independence. But the dog, with one eye ever on the audience, has been wheedled into slavery, and praised and patted into the renunciation of his nature. Once he ceased hunting and became man's plate-licker, the Rubicon was crossed. Thenceforth he was a gentleman of leisure; and except the few whom we keep working, the whole race grew more and more self-conscious, mannered and affected.

—Robert Louis Stevenson,
"The Character of Dogs"

The dog…commends himself to our favor by affording play to our propensity for mastery, and as he is also an item of expense, and commodity serves no industrial purpose, he holds a well-assured place in men's regard as a thing of good repute.

—Thorstein Veblen,
"The Theory of the Leisure Class"

[The dog] is the one species I wouldn't mind seeing vanish from the face of the earth. I wish they were like the white Rhino—six of them left in the Serengeti National Park, and all males.

—Alan Bennett, "Getting On"

But dog-haters are exceptional; I would almost write "freakish"; and their freakish hate is seldom inherited.

—Patsy Bloom, "Tails of the Unexpected"

I'll get you my pretty, and your little dog, too.

—Wicked Witch of the West
(Margaret Hamilton), *The Wizard of Oz*

Funny bone

Outside of a dog, a book is man's best friend. Inside of a dog it's too dark to read.

—GROUCHO MARX

My husband and I are either going to buy a dog or have a child. We can't decide whether to ruin our carpets or ruin our lives.

—RITA RUDNER

Asthma doesn't seem to bother me any more unless I'm around cigars or dogs. The thing that would bother me most would be a dog smoking a cigar.

—STEVE ALLEN

It's a dog eat dog world, and I'm wearing Milkbone underwear.

—NORM (George Wendt), *Cheers*

I bought a dog the other day... I named him Stay. It's fun to call him... "Come here, Stay! Come here, Stay!" He went insane. Now he just ignores me and keeps typing.

—STEVEN WRIGHT

Asking a working writer what he feels about critics is like asking a lamp-post how it feels about dogs.

—Christopher Hampton

I wonder if other dogs think poodles are members of a weird religious cult.

—Rita Rudner

Homer: Well crying isn't going to help. Now, you can sit there feeling sorry for yourself or you can eat can after can of dog food until your tears smell enough like dog food until your dog comes back, or you can go out there and find your dog.

Bart: You're right! (Gets up and leaves)

Homer: Rats! I almost had him eating dog food.

—Bart and Homer Simpson, *The Simpsons*

There is no doubt that a dog is loyal. But does that mean we should emulate him? After all, he is loyal to people, not to other dogs.

—KARL KRAUS,
Half-Truths and One-and-a-Half Truths

I'm not going to call a dog "Dog." I suppose if she were a baby you'd call her "Person."

—LOUISE BRYANT (Diane Keaton) to JOHN REED
(Warren Beatty), *Reds*

Now tell me, which one of these dogs would you want to have as your wide receiver on your football team?

—BUCK LAUGHLIN (Fred Willard), *Best in Show*

Being a childless woman of child-bearing age, I am a walking target for people's concerned analysis. No one looks at a single man with a Labrador Retriever and says, "Will you look at the way he throws the tennis ball to that dog? Now, there's a guy who wants to have a son."

—ANNE PATCHETT, "This Dog's Life"

Lassie looked brilliant, in part because the farm family she lived with was made up of idiots. Remember? One of them was always getting pinned under the tractor...

—DAVE BARRY

A Canadian psychologist is selling a video that teaches you how to test your dog's IQ. Here's how it works: if you spend $12.99 for the video, your dog is smarter than you.

—JAY LENO, *The Tonight Show with Jay Leno*